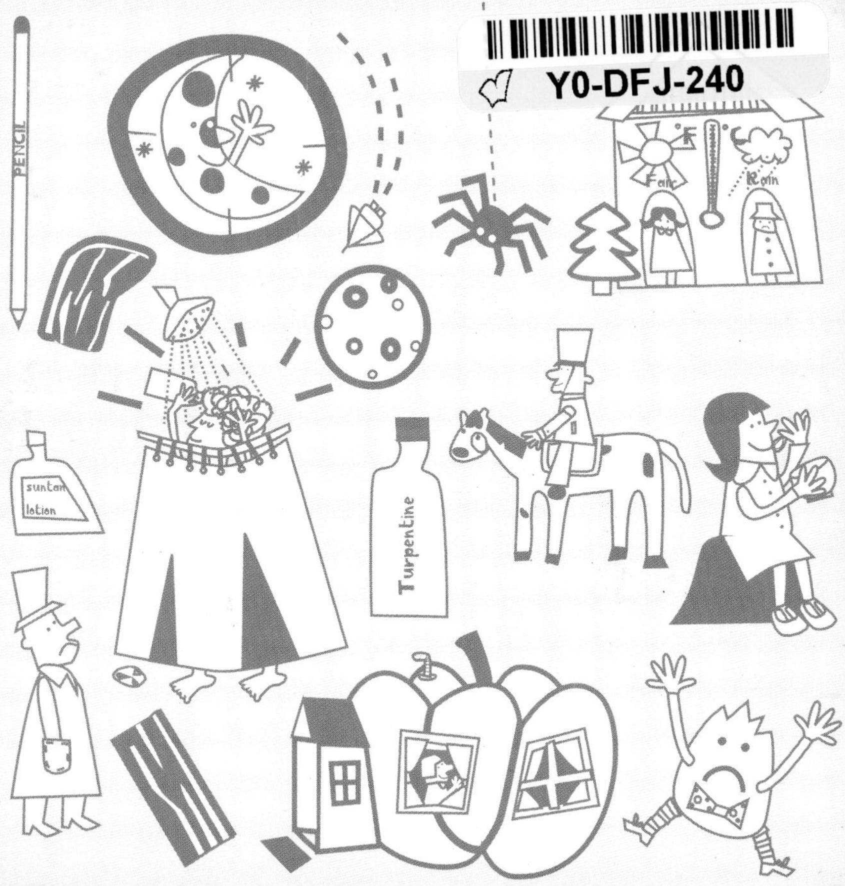
PENCIL
°F
°C
Fair
Rain
suntan
lotion
Turpentine

Copyright © 1997 by Nila Aye

First American Edition 1998 published by Orchard Books
First published in Great Britain in 1997 by Ragged Bears Publishing

All rights reserved. No part of this book may be reproduced or transmitted in any form or by any means, electronic or mechanical, including photocopying, recording, or by any information storage or retrieval system, without permission in writing from the Publisher.

Orchard Books
95 Madison Avenue
New York, NY 10016

Manufactured in Hong Kong
Book design by Nila Aye

10 9 8 7 6 5 4 3 2 1

dedicated to
CHLOE
my dog

Library of Congress Cataloging-in-Publication Data

Nila's little yellow book of nursery rhymes
    Orchard's little yellow book of nursery rhymes / by Nila Aye. — 1st American ed.
    p. cm.
    "First published in Great Britain in 1997 by Ragged Bears Publishing"—T.p. verso.
    Summary: Presents an illustrated collection of classic nursery rhymes.
    ISBN 0-531-30062-5
    1. Nursery rhymes. 2. Children's poetry. [1. Nursery rhymes.]
I. Aye, Nila, ill. II. Title.
PZ8.3.N56697 1998
398.8—dc21   97-12369

Orchard's Little Yellow Book of Nursery Rhymes

By NILA AYE

ORCHARD BOOKS • NEW YORK

Humpty Dumpty sat on a wall,
Humpty Dumpty had a great fall.

Ouch

All the King's horses
And all the King's men
Couldn't put Humpty together again.

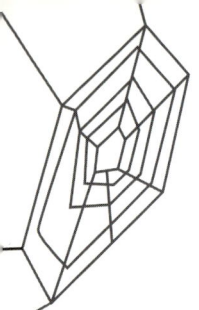

Little Miss Muffet

Sat on a tuffet,
Eating her curds and whey.

Hot Cross Buns

Hot Cross Buns

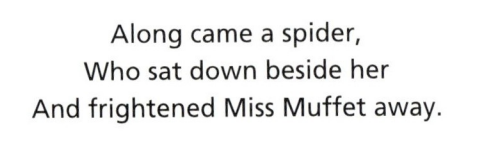

Along came a spider,
Who sat down beside her
And frightened Miss Muffet away.

All the King's horses
And all the King's men
Couldn't put Humpty together again.

Little Miss Muffet

Sat on a tuffet,
Eating her curds and whey.

Along came a spider,
Who sat down beside her
And frightened Miss Muffet away.

Hot Cross Buns

Hot Cro

yuck

Hot cross buns!
Hot cross buns!

One a penny, two a penny,
Hot cross buns!
If your daughters do not like them,
Give them to your sons.
One a penny, two a penny,
Hot cross buns!

yum-yum

Jack Sprat could eat no fat,

PENCIL

FAT

LEAN

CLEAN

His wife could eat no lean,
And so, between the two of them,
They licked the platter clean.

Baa, baa, black sheep,

Have you any wool?
Yes, sir, yes, sir,
Three bags full.

One for the master, And one for the dame,

And one for the little boy who lives down the lane.

NORTH

WEST

Gregory Griggs, Gregory Griggs

Had twenty-seven different wigs.
He wore them up, he wore them down,
To please the people of the town.
He wore them east, he wore them west,
But never could tell which one he loved best.

EAST

SOUTH

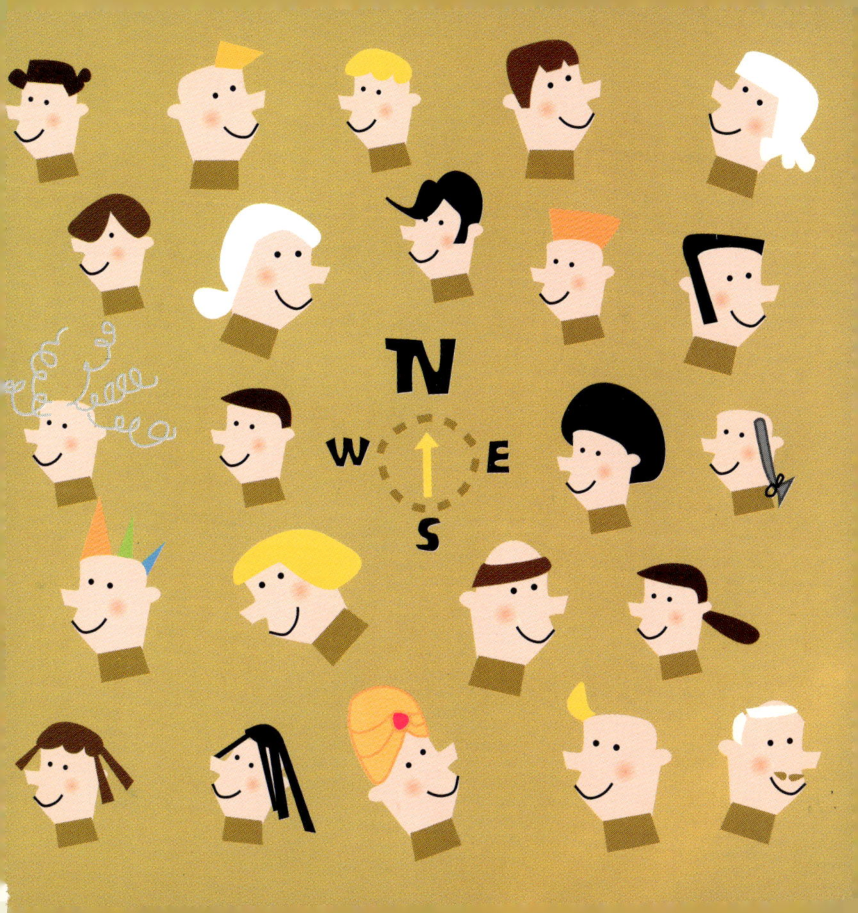
N
W
E
S

Queen Queen Caroline

Washed her hair in turpentine,
Turpentine to make it shine,

Queen Queen Caroline.

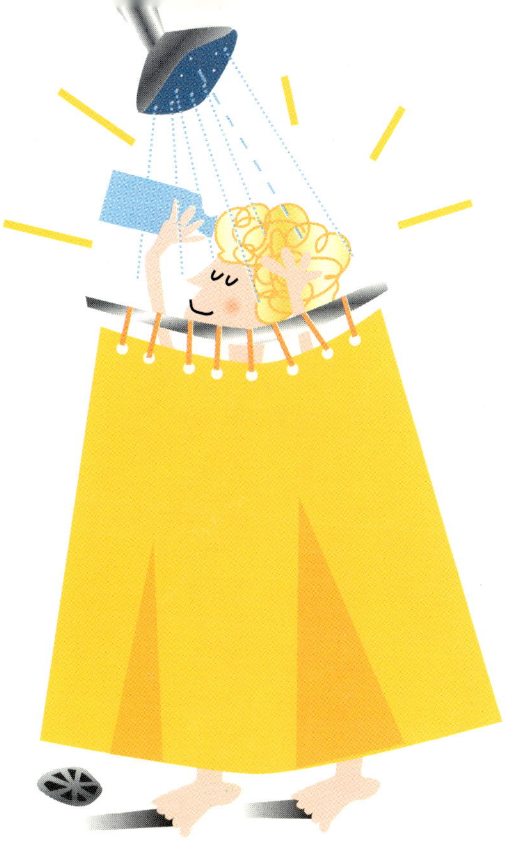

This little man lived all alone,

And he was a man of sorrow;
For, if the weather was fair today,
He was sure it would rain tomorrow.

sunglasses

suntan lotion

sun hat

TODAY tomorrow

Fair Rain

umbrella

rain boot

Hickory, dickory, dock,

The mouse ran up the clock.
The clock struck one,
The mouse ran down,

Hickory, dickory, dock.

up **down**

Peter, Peter, pumpkin eater,

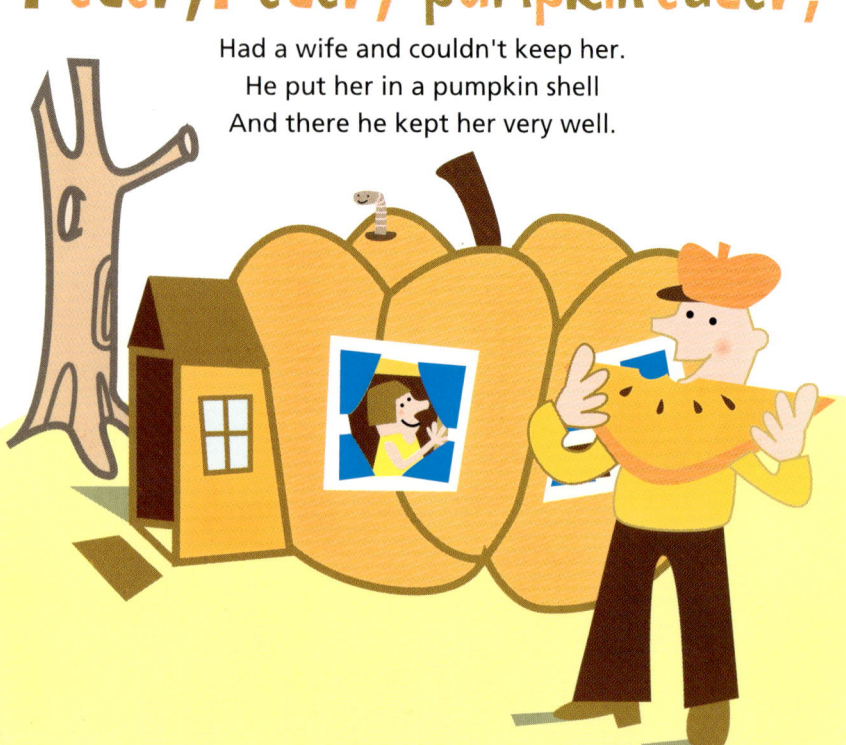

Had a wife and couldn't keep her.
He put her in a pumpkin shell
And there he kept her very well.

- pumpkin cookie
- pumpkin tea
- pumpkin ice cream
- pumpkin candy
- pumpkin cake
- pumpkin pie
- pumpkin soup
- pumpkin milkshake
- pumpkin sandwich

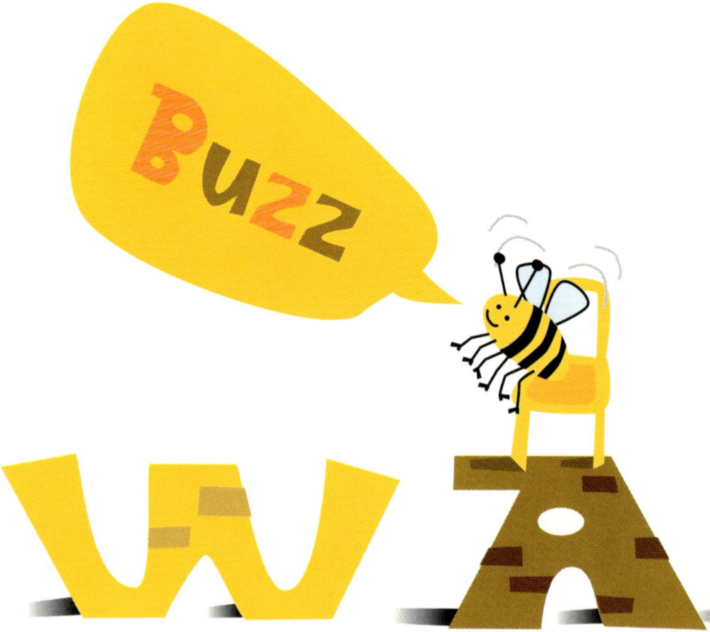
Buzz

There was a BEE
Sat on a wall.
"Buzz" said he,
And that was all.

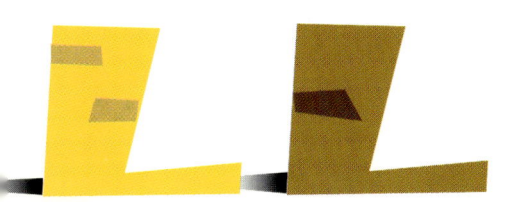

I see the moon,

And the moon sees me.
God bless the moon,
And God bless me.

star

view from telescope

moon

telescope

planets

flying saucer

rocket

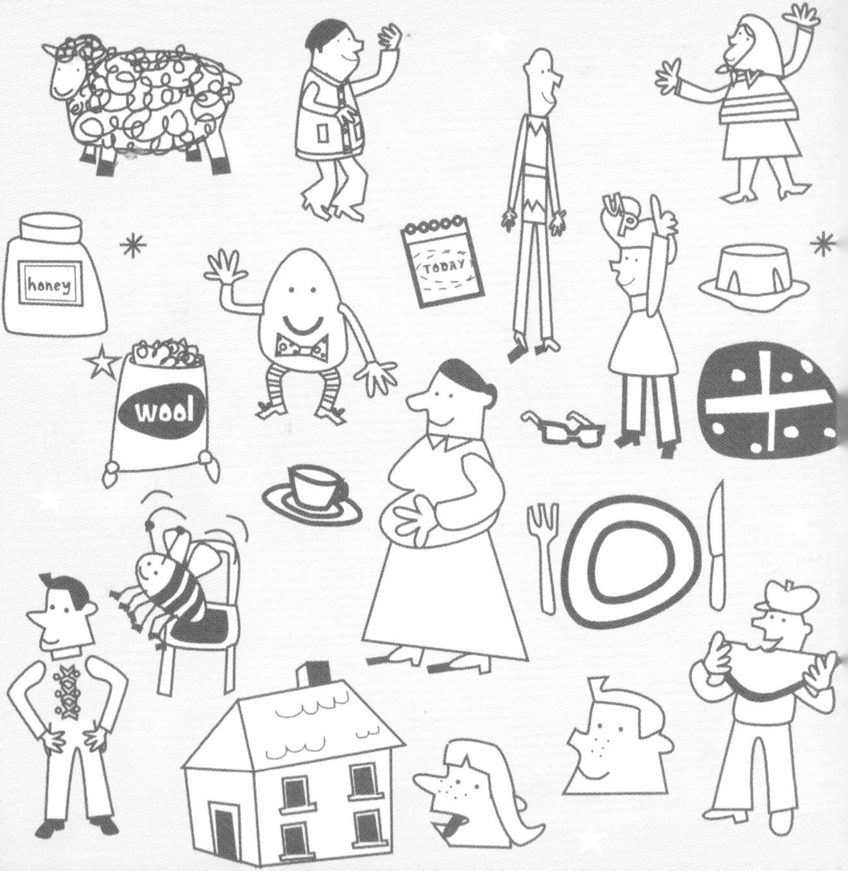
honey
TODAY
wool
UP